Reading Comprehension Workbook

Level 2

Series Designer
Philip J. Solimene

Editor
Sharon Diane Orlan

Reading Consultant
Sidney J. Rauch, Ed.D.
Professor of Reading and Education
Hofstra University, New York

EDCON

Story Authors

Ruth W. Barrett
Eleanor Coleman
Ellen Cummiskey
Jaskson Daviss
Walter Holden
Justine Kusner
Nancy Byrnes Martel
Jacqueline Nightingale

Printed in U.S.A.
ISBN# 0-931334-44-6

CONTENTS

CONTENTS

Three Jobs for Three Brothers

Learn the Key Words

brother   (bruŦH′ ər)   a boy who has the same father and mother as another boy or girl
> *Jack and his <u>brother</u> went to the store.*

carry   (ker′ ē)   to take from one place to another
> *Mary could not <u>carry</u> the box by herself.*

drop   (drop)   to let something fall
> *Do not <u>drop</u> those eggs, or they will break.*

land   (land)   a country or place where people live; the parts of the earth not covered by water
> *They live in a far away <u>land</u>.*

sent   (sent)   to have someone or something go somewhere
> *Her mother <u>sent</u> her to buy some milk.*

wear   (wer, war)   to have on; to put on
> *Ellen likes to <u>wear</u> her new shoes to school.*

Preview:

1. Read the title.
2. Look at the picture.
3. Read the first three paragraphs of the story.
4. Then answer the following question.

You learned from your preview that
_____ a. the three sons lived far away from their mother.
_____ b. the mother asked them for three peacocks.
_____ c. the woman's sons wanted to leave home.
_____ d. the woman gave each son a new basket.

Turn to the Comprehension Check on page 4 for the right answer.

Now read the story.

Read to find out about growing up.

Three Jobs for Three Brothers

Before these boys leave home, they must each do three things to prove they are ready.

Some Things You Will Read About:

peacock (pē´kok) a bird with a beautiful blue, green and gold tail
princess (prin´ses) a woman who is the daughter of a king and queen

---

Three Jobs for Three Brothers

Once, in a faraway land, there was a woman who had three sons.

She said to them, "You all want to go away from home. But first, you must each bring me three things. They are: a fan made from the tail of a peacock for me to wear, a new basket to carry to market, and a fire that will never go out."

Then she gave them each a small chest of money.

The first son said, "But, Mother, there are no peacocks in all the land."

The next son said, "But, Mother, it is too cold to get straw to make baskets."

The other son, Jack, said nothing.

Their mother laughed. "You can find straw and peacocks if you try." And she sent them away.

In town, two of the brothers knew two girls. Each girl had a father who helped the two brothers. But Jack had no one to help him.

The girls' fathers sent the two brothers away. When they came back, the girls made fans from the peacock feathers.

The two brothers needed straw to make baskets. The girls told them of a farmer who had some. When they brought back the straw, the girls made the baskets.

Jack still had nothing. He wanted to get his mother a fan to wear and a new basket to carry, but he didn't know what to do. And since he had nothing, he would never get away from home.

At the river, he sat down and cried.

A frog was sitting by the river. It asked, "Why are you crying?"

Jack told the story.

The frog said, "There is a country on the other side of that mountain where there are peacocks. Bring some back to me. Then go down the road, where you will find a field of tall grass that has dried. Bring some of that back, too." Then the frog told him to come back the next day.

When he got home, his brothers did not look happy.

They said, "It is a trick. There is no fire that will never go out. Mother sent us to find something that cannot be found."

In the morning, Jack went back to the river. He told the frog what his brothers had said.

The frog said, "It is not a trick. The sun is the fire that will never go out. You must carry me up into the honey tree. But do not drop me. Then, you must say the words that I tell you."

Jack did as he was told.

Then he saw a ball of fire over his head, and he saw the frog turn into a beautiful girl.

She told him that she was really a princess. "Drop the ball of fire into your bag. I will make a fan and a basket for you. Then we will go to your mother," she told him.

When they got back home, his mother was very pleased. Then Jack and the beautiful princess went off, hand in hand.

3

Three Jobs for Three Brothers

COMPREHENSION CHECK

Choose the best answer.

1. The three boys had to find three things
    _____ a.   before they could leave home.
    _____ b.   to make a fire with.
    _____ c.   so their mother could go away.
    _____ d.   to make some money.

2. Jack's mother
    _____ a.   did not like the frog.
    _____ b.   helped the boys go away.
    _____ c.   did not want her boys to leave.
    _____ d.   picked the boys' friends for them.

3. The two brothers
    _____ a.   found everything on their own.
    _____ b.   got help from two girls.
    _____ c.   did not find anything.
    _____ d.   were happy with their lives.

4. The feathers had to come from a
    _____ a.   duck.
    _____ b.   robin.
    _____ c.   pigeon.
    _____ d.   peacock.

5. The frog turned into a
    _____ a.   boy.
    _____ b.   princess.
    _____ c.   mother.
    _____ d.   father.

6. The fire that never went out, was
    _____ a.   the sun.
    _____ b.   the moon.
    _____ c.   in the tree.
    _____ d.   in the water.

7. Jack's brothers
    _____ a.   knew where to find the fire.
    _____ b.   thought their mother was tricking them.
    _____ c.   wanted to work in the town near the girls.
    _____ d.   liked to take long walks through the woods.

8. Before he met the frog, Jack was
    _____ a.   happy.
    _____ b.   sad.
    _____ c.   pleased.
    _____ d.   angry.

9. Another name for this story could be
    _____ a.   "Fun in the Woods."
    _____ b.   "A Happy Family."
    _____ c.   "Going Out Into the World."
    _____ d.   "Building a House."

10. This story is mainly about
    _____ a.   a frog who helps a young boy.
    _____ b.   two brothers and their different ways.
    _____ c.   growing up in the old days.
    _____ d.   helping and being helped.

Check your answers with the key on page 53.

Idea Starter: What other problems do young people have as they grow up?

Three Jobs for Three Brothers

VOCABULARY CHECK

brother	carry	drop	land	sent	wear

I. *Fill in the blank in each sentence with the correct key word from the box above.*

1. Try not to _____ your mother's glasses.

2. The store _____ a box to our house.

3. That box is too heavy to _____ .

4. My mother told me to _____ my hat to school.

5. Karen and her _____ walked to the park.

6. The people who live next door came from a far away _____ .

II. *Use the words from the box to fill in the puzzle.*

Down

1. a boy who has the same mother and father as another boy or girl

6. a country

Across

2. to have on

3. to have someone or something go somewhere

4. to take from one place to another

5. to let something fall

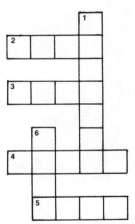

Check your answers with the key on page 55.

The Fox Show

Learn the Key Words

cage	(kāj)	a place with bars to keep animals in *The bear was in a cage at the zoo.*
done	(dun)	to finish something *When Mary was done with her homework, she went out to play.*
drive	(drīv)	to make a car, bus or truck go along *Mother will drive us to the park.*
follow	(fol′ ō)	to go after someone or something *Jack's dog may follow him to school again.*
fox	(foks)	a wild animal like a dog, but with a long, bushy tail *The fox wags its tail like a dog, when it is happy.*
knock	(nok)	1. to bang on something and make a noise *I heard a knock on the door.* 2. to hit or bump into something *The cat tried to knock over the dish.*

Preview:
1. Read the title.
2. Look at the picture.
3. Read the first five paragraphs of the story.
4. Then answer the following question.

You learned from your preview that
_____ a. Mrs. Wilson drove the children to the zoo.
_____ b. the children would not see many animals at the zoo.
_____ c. Bobby was looking forward to going to the zoo.
_____ d. Mr. Jones was the teacher.
Turn to the Comprehension Check on page 9 for the right answer.

Now read the story.

Read to find out about an animal with a sense of humor.

The Fox Show

Bobby thinks the red fox is the most interesting animal at the zoo. He learns that it has a good sense of humor, too.

Something You Will Read About:

tiger (tī′gər)   a large wild animal with stripes, belonging to the cat family

The Fox Show

Bobby was happy when he left for school this morning. His class was going to the zoo. He hurried to the bus stop. Soon, the big yellow bus came.

"Are you going to drive us to the zoo, Mr. Jones?" Bobby asked.

"Yes, but first I will drive you to school. From there, we will go to the zoo," Mr. Jones said.

At school, Mrs. Wilson showed the children pictures of different animals.

She told them, "You will see many animals at the zoo. Look closely at all the animals. Think of the one you like best. Then you can tell us about it tomorrow."

When they got to the zoo. Mrs. Wilson said, "Follow me. Stay close and no one will get lost."

First, they saw the bears. Then, they went to see the tigers. Near the tigers' cage, they saw five monkeys playing tag. Next, they saw a red fox. Its tail was very thick. Bobby liked the fox best of all and he stayed at the fox cage for a long time.

He heard a knock and saw a man with a pail of water and a wooden box going into the cage.

The man told Bobby that he was going to give the fox lunch, and Bobby could watch.

First, the man gave the fox water. When the man bent over to put the pail down, his hat came off, but he didn't know it. When the fox was done drinking, it tried to knock the pail over. Bobby saw everything the fox had done. When the man was ready to go, he put his hand on his head to fix his hat, but it was gone. He looked in his pocket and then he looked all around the cage. But the hat was nowhere in sight. Then the man pulled some meat from the box. The fox ran over quickly, and while it was eating, the man looked for his hat again. Soon, he saw his hat under the rock and pulled it out. As he was putting it on, he asked Bobby, "Did you see the fox trick me?"

"Yes, I saw the tricky fox," laughed Bobby.

"Are you here alone?" the man asked.

Bobby said, "No," but he looked around and saw that everyone had gone.

"Follow me," the man said. They walked past many cages and soon Bobby saw Mrs. Wilson and the children.

"Where were you?" she asked. "We have all been looking for you."

"I was watching the fox show," said Bobby.

Just then, Mr. Jones came along.

"You were on time for the bus this morning, but you are late for lunch," he laughed.

Bobby laughed, too, and then sat down to eat lunch. He was very happy that he saw the tricky fox. He would have a good story to tell the class tomorrow.

The Fox Show

COMPREHENSION CHECK

Choose the best answer.

1.   Bobby was happy because
_____ a.   his class was going to the zoo.
_____ b.   he was going to tell a story.
_____ c.   his mother was driving him to school.
_____ d.   he liked to talk to the bus driver.

2.   The children stayed close to Mrs. Wilson
_____ a.   because they liked her.
_____ b.   so they wouldn't get lost.
_____ c.   because the man told them to.
_____ d.   so they could see the animals.

3.   Bobby stopped to watch the
_____ a.   bear.
_____ b.   monkeys.
_____ c.   fox.
_____ d.   tigers.

4.   The man went into the fox cage to
_____ a.   give the fox lunch.
_____ b.   clean the fox cage.
_____ c.   look for something.
_____ d.   take the fox out.

5.   The fox was tricky because he
_____ a.   found the man's hat.
_____ b.   liked to stand on his head.
_____ c.   liked to play behind rocks.
_____ d.   hid the man's hat.

6.   The man put the meat out for the fox
_____ a.   because he was being nice to the animal.
_____ b.   to keep the fox busy while he looked for **his hat.**
_____ c.   to make friends with the tricky fox.
_____ d.   because he wanted the fox to talk.

7.   If it weren't for the man in the fox cage,
_____ a.   the children wouldn't have seen the show.
_____ b.   the fox would have had his lunch early.
_____ c.   the zoo would have closed before lunch.
_____ d.   Bobby would have been lost at the zoo.

8.   Bobby
_____ a.   was not happy that he saw the tricky fox.
_____ b.   would tell his class about the fox the next day.
_____ c.   did not have a good story to tell his friends.
_____ d.   did not want to find his class again.

9.   Another name for this story could be
_____ a.   "A Day at the Zoo."
_____ b.   "Bears Are Fun."
_____ c.   "A Tricky Monkey."
_____ d.   "Losing a Hat."

10.   This story is mainly about
_____ a.   a class trip to the zoo.
_____ b.   looking for a child's lost hat.
_____ c.   seeing a tricky fox at the zoo.
_____ d.   making friends with zoo animals.

Check your answers with the key on page 53.

Idea Starter: What animals do you remember from visiting the zoo?

The Fox Show

VOCABULARY CHECK

| cage | done | drive | follow | fox | knock |

I. **Fill in the blank in each sentence with the correct key word from the box above.**

1. We saw the monkeys in their _____ at the zoo.
2. I _____ my mother when we walk through the stores.
3. I like to _____ the bumper cars at the park.
4. A _____ has a long tail.
5. When I was _____ setting the table, we ate dinner.
6. We heard a _____ on the window and there was my friend Sam.

II. **Find the hidden words in the letters below. They may be written from left to right or up and down. One word, that is not a key word, has been done for you.**

C	A	G	E	M	O	P	S
Z	E	B	R	A	T	O	O
D	S	F	O	X	A	B	C
R	T	O	U	N	D	E	R
I	B	L	M	S	E	N	K
V	I	L	K	A	A	U	N
E	A	O	P	L	U	N	O
B	P	W	D	O	N	E	C
A	C	E	R	T	L	A	K

Check your answers with the key on page 55.

This page may be reproduced for classroom use.

Getting to Know Each Other

Learn the Key Words

family	(fam′ ə lē)	a mother, father and their children *There are six people in Caroline's family.*
reach	(rēch)	to touch; to stretch out *James could not reach the cookie jar on the table.*
stand	(stand)	to be on your feet *MaryAnn had to stand and face the class when she read.*
threw	(thrü)	to send up into the air; past tense of throw *Mike threw the ball to Larry.*
wait	(wāt)	to stay in one spot until someone comes or something happens *Lucy had to wait for her brother to take her to school.*
write	(rīt)	to form words by putting letters down on paper or a board *Susan had to write her homework on the blackboard.*

Preview:

1. Read the title.
2. Look at the picture.
3. Read the first six paragraphs of the story.
4. Then answer the following question.

You learned from your preview that
____ a. Marty and Chrissy had been friends for a long time.
____ b. Chrissy was mad at Marty.
____ c. Marty kept asking Chrissy questions.
____ d. Marty was afraid to ask Chrissy something.
Turn to the Comprehension Check on page 14 for the right answer.

Now read the story.

Read to find out about making new friends.

Getting to Know Each Other

Marty and Chrissy had not known each other very long, but they were already becoming good friends.

Something You Will Read About:

wheelchair (hwēl´cher)   a chair with wheels used by people who cannot use their legs

Getting to Know Each Other

Marty and Chrissy had just met. So far, each had found out the other's family name and each could see what the other looked like. These were good things to know, but Marty had another question. He just could not ask it.

"Why not?" Chrissy asked.

"I don't think you would like me any more," said Marty.

Nothing Chrissy said could make Marty ask his question, so Chrissy tried to guess.

"I think you want to know about my chair and you want to know why it has wheels. Well, a chair with wheels can take me where I want to go. Does that answer your question?" she asked.

Marty said it didn't, but he still would not tell what his question was.

Chrissy said, "Wait! You want to know why I ride around in a wheelchair. I can't stand or walk, Marty. I can't reach things high up because my legs don't work. Was that what you wanted to know?"

"No," said Marty.

Chrissy was surprised. "I will guess once more," she said. "Do you want to know what it is like for me? There are many games I can't play and I will never stand or dance. That is the way things are and I can't

do much about it. But just because I can't walk, doesn't mean I can't do anything. I go where I want to go. Other people can give me a ride in my chair or I can work the wheels with my hands to make it go. I can do many things with friends like you. I can write and as you see, I can play this game of trying to guess your question. Now tell me, did I guess right?"

The answer was still no.

"Marty, I will not be angry. Please tell me. You can even write it down if you like. I am all out of guesses!" Chrissy said with a laugh. She threw a ball to him.

Marty started to talk about other things. Then, he asked, "I want to know if I may have a ride."

"A ride?" Chrissy did not know what Marty was thinking about.

"I want to ride in your chair," said Marty. "It looks like a good game."

He threw the ball back to Chrissy.

Chrissy began to laugh and Marty was happy that she was not angry after all. Then she showed Marty how to help her reach from her chair to one without wheels. Marty could not wait to sit in her chair. She

showed him how to work the wheels. He went from room to room as Chrissy looked on. They laughed so hard that the girl's family came in to see what was so funny.

There was Chrissy, sitting on one chair, having a fine time, while Marty sat in the chair with the wheels. He looked so sleepy!

"I found out what Marty wanted to know," said Chrissy.

Then Marty had another question. "Why is Chrissy so much better at this than I am? This is hard work for me!"

Getting to Know Each Other

COMPREHENSION CHECK

Choose the best answer.

1. Chrissy
    _____ a. could not have any fun.
    _____ b. could not get around.
    _____ c. did not have any friends.
    _____ d. felt good about herself.

2. Chrissy was in a chair with wheels because she
    _____ a. could not walk.
    _____ b. could not talk.
    _____ c. could not play games.
    _____ d. didn't like walking.

3. At first, Marty
    _____ a. did not like Chrissy.
    _____ b. thought that Chrissy did not like him.
    _____ c. would not ask his question.
    _____ d. played some games with Chrissy.

4. Chrissy
    _____ a. was able to take things the way they were.
    _____ b. cried about not being able to run.
    _____ c. did not like Marty because he could walk.
    _____ d. hoped someone could make her better.

5. It was important for Chrissy to
    _____ a. have only one friend.
    _____ b. do things for herself.
    _____ c. do only quiet things.
    _____ d. stay in her chair all the time.

6. Marty was afraid to ask Chrissy
    _____ a. why she was in a chair with wheels.
    _____ b. if she would ever be able to walk.
    _____ c. if he could have a ride in her chair.
    _____ d. what it felt like not to be able to walk.

7. Chrissy
    _____ a. enjoyed seeing Marty have fun in her chair.
    _____ b. felt badly about Marty riding in her chair.
    _____ c. did not let Marty use her chair.
    _____ d. was afraid her family would be angry.

8. Marty
    _____ a. saw that it was not easy to be in Chrissy's place.
    _____ b. did not want to be Chrissy's friend anymore.
    _____ c. believed that Chrissy was smarter than he.
    _____ d. wanted to get a chair like Chrissy's for his very own.

9. Another name for this story could be
    _____ a. "Friends."
    _____ b. "Family."
    _____ c. "Spring Fun."
    _____ d. "School Days."

10. This story is mainly about
    _____ a. a sad girl in a chair with wheels.
    _____ b. a family who takes good care of their child.
    _____ c. a fresh boy with no feelings.
    _____ d. friends understanding each other.

Check your answers with the key on page 53.

Idea Starter: How would you feel if you were in Chrissy's place?

Getting to Know Each Other

VOCABULARY CHECK

family	reach	stand	threw	wait	write

I. Fill in the blank in each sentence with the correct key word from the box above.

1. My _____ went on a trip this summer.

2. I have to _____ a letter to my friend.

3. It's hard for me to _____ the books when they are on the high shelf.

4. We _____ in line at the movies on Saturday afternoons.

5. Paul _____ his hat up into the air.

6. I _____ for the bus at the corner.

II. Fill in the blanks in the story with the words from the box.

Chrissy tried to guess what Marty wanted to ask her. When she could not _____ any more, she asked him to _____ it down. But Marty was still afraid. Chrissy told him she could not _____ or _____ things high up. But that was not what Marty wanted to know. Chrissy _____ a ball to Marty. Then Marty had a ride in her chair. Marty got what he wanted. They both laughed so hard that Chrissy's _____ came in to see what was so much fun.

Check your answers with the key on page 56.

This page may be reproduced for classroom use.

the unicorn

Learn the Key Words

drink	(dringk)	to swallow something like water or milk *I like to <u>drink</u> milk.*
face	(fās)	the front of your head *The look on Jim's <u>face</u> told us that he was happy.*
foot	(fu̇t)	the part of your body at the end of your leg *Janet fell and hurt her <u>foot</u>.*
kind	(kīnd)	to do good; be nice *The old woman was <u>kind</u> to animals.*
king	(king)	a man who is the head of a country *The <u>king</u> ruled the country for many years.*
love	(luv)	a strong liking for someone or something *Peter has a great <u>love</u> for reading books.*

Preview:

1. Read the title.
2. Look at the picture.
3. Read the first five paragraphs of the story.
4. Then answer the following question.

You learned from your preview that
_____ a. King Totwotoo was a very kind man.
_____ b. King Totwotoo wanted the unicorn for himself.
_____ c. King Totwotoo cared about other people's happiness.
_____ d. King Totwotoo liked unicorns as pets.
Turn to the Comprehension Check on page 19 for the right answer.

Now read the story.
Read to find out about a different and powerful animal.

the UNICORN

Unicorns were said to have magical powers—and if a man had the unicorn's horn, he could rule the world.

Some Things You Will Read About:

unicorn (yü′nə kôrn)   a make-believe animal like a horse, but with a horn on its head

horn (hôrn)   a hard, pointed growth on an animal's head

the unicorn

Once in a faraway land there lived a very bad king. His name was Totwotoo. When he found that there was a unicorn in his land, he called all of his people together.

He told them, "I want that unicorn!"

"You will have it," they said. "We will catch it before dark."

Now, the unicorn was very strong and it could run faster than any other animal. On its head, it had one pretty horn. This horn was wanted by many. It could also make all things good. If a man had one, he could be loved by all.

King Totwotoo wanted the horn for himself.

His men looked all over for the unicorn. Just before dark, one of the men saw it.

"Look! Over there!"

The others turned and saw the unicorn.

"But how will we catch it?" they asked each other.

They sat under a tree to think. They saw the unicorn playing with the little animals. The unicorn put its horn in the water, then took a drink. Very soon after, the unicorn went to sleep.

The men ran to catch it while it slept. The unicorn jumped. The men did not have the might to hold it. It stamped its foot and ran off.

When the men got back to town, the first man told King Totwotoo all about the unicorn.

Then another told him, "It was a pretty picture to see. The animals all walked with the unicorn and the birds were singing to it. There was love all around."

King Totwotoo listened. Then, he stopped to think.

"It likes singing, does it," said the King.

Now King Totwotoo had a little girl. She was very kind and she could sing as pretty as any bird. He told her about the unicorn, but said nothing about the horn.

"I will go alone and sing for it, Daddy," she said, her face shining.

But then she asked, "Please Daddy, if it comes, may I have it for my pet?"

"Yes, yes," he said to her, but told his men, "Stay with her and bring me that horn!"

The next day the little girl went to find the unicorn. She stopped by the river to drink the cool water. She sat in the flowers and sang. Then, she heard footsteps behind her. She turned her face and saw the snow-white unicorn.

She laughed and talked to it, saying, "Kind unicorn, please do come home with me."

The unicorn walked with her. The animals walked with them, too. And the birds sang all the way home.

The men King Totwotoo had told to go with her, were in the flowers behind the trees. They saw everything, but did nothing. Her song was stronger than their might. They saw King Totwotoo running to put one arm around his little girl, and the other around the horn.

Then, the men were surprised. The unicorn looked at King Totwotoo and the King looked at the unicorn. For the first time, he saw how very pretty the animal was. The horn had made the bad king good.

the unicorn

COMPREHENSION CHECK

Choose the best answer.

1. The king wanted the unicorn for
    _____ a.   its horn.
    _____ b.   a pet.
    _____ c.   a friend.
    _____ d.   his daughter.

2. The unicorn's horn
    _____ a.   would not work without the unicorn.
    _____ b.   could make all things good.
    _____ c.   would bring rain to the land.
    _____ d.   could make all things bad.

3. The animals in the woods
    _____ a.   were afraid of the unicorn.
    _____ b.   never saw the unicorn.
    _____ c.   helped the unicorn get away.
    _____ d.   loved the unicorn.

4. The unicorn was
    _____ a.   mean and fresh.
    _____ b.   an ugly animal.
    _____ c.   sweet and kind.
    _____ d.   not very friendly.

5. The king's little girl
    _____ a.   wanted to get the unicorn's horn.
    _____ b.   knew about her father's plan.
    _____ c.   wanted the unicorn for a pet.
    _____ d.   did not believe her father.

6. The unicorn came over to the little girl because
    _____ a.   she looked sad.
    _____ b.   he wanted her to take him home.
    _____ c.   she set out food.
    _____ d.   he heard her song.

7. The king's men
    _____ a.   were able to get the unicorn's horn.
    _____ b.   were won over by the girl's song.
    _____ c.   killed the unicorn.
    _____ d.   ran back to their homes.

8. The bad king
    _____ a.   was made kind by the unicorn.
    _____ b.   took the horn off the unicorn.
    _____ c.   did not care about his little girl.
    _____ d.   never gave orders to his people.

9. Another name for this story could be
    _____ a.   "A King Changes."
    _____ b.   "A Run in the Forest."
    _____ c.   "Singing for Your Supper."
    _____ d.   "A Pet for the King."

10. This story is mainly about
    _____ a.   a mean king.
    _____ b.   the love a unicorn brought.
    _____ c.   a sad little girl.
    _____ d.   the strength of the king's men.

Check your answers with the key on page 53.

Idea Starter: Why do you think the king was mean and greedy?

the unicorn

VOCABULARY CHECK

drink	face	foot	kind	king	love

I. **Fill in the blank in each sentence with the correct key word from the box above.**

1. I could tell by the look on her _____, that she was going to cry.

2. The _____ man helped me cross the busy street.

3. On a hot day, I like to _____ something cold.

4. The _____ wore a beautiful crown.

5. I was walking without shoes and I cut my _____ on a piece of glass.

6. I _____ to go out walking with my mother and father.

II. **Are the key words used the way they should be? Check yes or no.**

1. A <u>foot</u> is at the end of a leg.   Yes _____   No _____

2. A <u>kind</u> child is mean to others.   Yes _____   No _____

3. I like to <u>drink</u> meat.   Yes _____   No _____

4. A <u>king</u> should care about his people.   Yes _____   No _____

5. A <u>face</u> can show many feelings.   Yes _____   No _____

6. Children <u>love</u> to play games.   Yes _____   No _____

Check your answers with the key on page 56.

A Whale of a Tale

Learn the Key Words

band   (band)
1. a long, thin piece of paper or cloth used as a trim
   She put a <u>band</u> around the edge of the book.
2. a group of people together (playing music or acting)
   We heard the school <u>band</u> playing some new songs.

crawl   (krôl)
to move along slowly, using your hands and feet like a baby
Tim had to <u>crawl</u> to get a puppy from under the house.

listen   (lis′n)
to hear things
<u>Listen</u>! Did you hear that strange noise?

visit   (viz′it)
to go to see someone, or be with people for a little while
We are going to <u>visit</u> Grandma and Grandpa today.

whale   (hwāl)
a very large animal, shaped like a fish, that lives in the ocean
A <u>whale</u> can be very friendly and very smart.

world   (wėrld)
the earth
Someday, I would like to take a trip around the <u>world</u>.

Preview:
1. Read the title.
2. Look at the picture.
3. Read the first six paragraphs of the story.
4. Then answer the following question.

You learned from your preview that
_____ a. Polly named her boat "CALIFORNIA."
_____ b. a whale was near Polly's boat.
_____ c. Polly's family visited the Whale family each year.
_____ d. the whale was not as big as Polly's boat.
Turn to the Comprehension Check on page 24 for the right answer.

Now read the story.

Read to find out about one of the largest animals in the world.

A Whale of a Tale

Even though whales are the largest animals in the world, they are very friendly and smart.

A Place You Will Read About:

California (kal ə fôr nyə) a western state in the United States

A Whale of a Tale

When Polly got her boat, she painted a big red band around it. For a name, she painted in big letters, "MY BOAT."

Day after day, she fished near her home in southern California.

Polly was in her pretty new boat all alone, when she saw something under the water. It was coming right at her!

It looked like a fish, but it was as big as a school bus. Polly moved quickly to try to get away.

It was coming faster. She was going to try to crawl down in the boat and hold on with her hands and feet, but when she stopped moving, the fish stopped, too.

Polly sat up to look and listen. She thought of what her father had told her last night. She was not supposed to go fishing alone because whales visit this place each year, about this time.

Now, she listened, but could not hear anything. When she saw its tail, though, she knew it was very near.

Then, what a surprise! She pulled in a big fish. She put the line in the water again and got another as big as the one before. This happened again and again.

But now it was time to go home. She started to row away. The whale came alongside her little boat again, but not fast. Polly put her hand on its head, and he liked her!

"I am going to name you William," Polly laughed, when she found out that sometimes whales can be friendly.

The next morning, William met her again, and each morning after. And each day she got another good catch.

Now, Polly was catching many more fish than Tim, her brother. He asked, "Where do you find so many fish?"

"My friend William helps me."

"Who is William?"

"Just a friend."

"You know you are not supposed to go out alone or with any people we don't know, and I am going to tell."

"Tell, tell, Tim will tell," sang Polly, as she walked away with her basket of fish.

Then, one night, Polly's father said, "It is time for the whales to visit other waters in other parts of the world. Soon, they will be gone."

Polly wanted to cry.

The next day, the sky was dark. A storm was coming up. It was not a good day to go out in a boat, but Polly had to see William one last time.

Out on the black water, her little boat moved up and down. Water began to fill her boat and started to cover her. All of a sudden, Polly felt something under her boat. It was William! She crawled onto his back and held on tight.

That night, MY BOAT, with its big red band, was nowhere to be found. Tim found Polly on the beach, walking home.

Everyone wanted to know how she made it through the storm with no help. But Polly would not tell. You know, most people in this world don't know much about whales. They would think it was just a story she had made up.

A Whale of a Tale

COMPREHENSION CHECK

Choose the best answer.

1. The name of Polly's boat was
    ____ a.   RED BAND.
    ____ b.   MY BOAT.
    ____ c.   DAD'S GIRL.
    ____ d.   LITTLE FISH.

2. Polly
    ____ a.   never went fishing alone.
    ____ b.   gave some fish to her brother.
    ____ c.   did not listen to her father.
    ____ d.   was never afraid in the water.

3. William was
    ____ a.   Polly's brother.
    ____ b.   a shark.
    ____ c.   Polly's father.
    ____ d.   a whale.

4. When William was near Polly's boat,
    ____ a.   he wanted to hurt the little girl.
    ____ b.   Polly caught more fish.
    ____ c.   he wanted to tip the boat over.
    ____ d.   Polly caught no fish at all.

5. Whales are
    ____ a.   sometimes friendly.
    ____ b.   never friendly.
    ____ c.   always mean.
    ____ d.   always friendly.

6. Polly should
    ____ a.   not have gone out on the water on a dark day.
    ____ b.   have tried to save her boat in the storm.
    ____ c.   go out alone in her boat all the time.
    ____ d.   never wear a life jacket on the boat.

7. Polly was saved from the storm by
    ____ a.   the low water.
    ____ b.   William.
    ____ c.   her brother.
    ____ d.   her boat.

8. People
    ____ a.   are always right about what they believe.
    ____ b.   always go fishing in storms.
    ____ c.   never take any chances.
    ____ d.   are often afraid of what they don't understand.

9. Another name for this story could be
    ____ a.   "A New Boat."
    ____ b.   "A Basket of Fish."
    ____ c.   "A Friendly Catch."
    ____ d.   "Storms at Sea."

10. This story is mainly about
    ____ a.   a family that goes fishing together.
    ____ b.   a little girl and her different friend.
    ____ c.   a boat with a red band.
    ____ d.   a terrible storm at sea.

Check your answers with the key on page 53.

Idea Starter: What else do you know about whales?

A Whale of a Tale

VOCABULARY CHECK

| band | crawl | listen | visit | whale | world |

I. **Fill in the blank in each sentence with the correct key word from the box above.**

1. I saw a _____ at the water show.

2. The children _____ to their teacher at school.

3. The baby began to _____ around the living room floor.

4. John plays the drums in his new _____ .

5. I like to _____ my friend across town.

6. I saw pictures of children from around the _____ .

II. **Match the words with their meanings by writing the letter of the right meaning next to each word.**

_____ 1. whale   a. a group of people together

_____ 2. band   b. to go to see someone or something

_____ 3. crawl   c. an animal that lives in the ocean

_____ 4. world   d. the earth

_____ 5. listen   e. to move along slowly, using hands and feet

_____ 6. visit   f. to hear things

Check your answers with the key on page 57.

A Gift From the Sea

Learn the Key Words

branch   (branch)   a part of a tree
The bird sat on a high branch.

need   (nēd)   to be in want of; cannot do without
You need a warm coat when the weather gets cold.

smell   (smel)   what your nose does
I can smell fish near the sea.

strong   (strông)   1.   to be able to lift or carry heavy things
My brother is a strong person.
2.   able to last a long time
The thought was still strong in my mind.

supper   (sup′pər)   evening meal
Mother cooked chicken for supper.

wonderful   (wun′dər fəl)   very good
Jean had a wonderful time at the circus.

Preview:
1.   Read the title.
2.   Look at the picture.
3.   Read the first nine paragraphs of the story.
4.   Then answer the following question.

You learned from your preview that
_____ a.   Reggie did not want Sparky's help.
_____ b.   Reggie and his friends were gathering reeds.
_____ c.   Reggie is telling the story to Sparky.
_____ d.   Reggie and Sparky understand each other.
Turn to the Comprehension Check on page 29 for the right answer.

Now read the story.

Read to find out about a boy who is close to nature.

A Gift From the Sea

One day at the ocean, Reggie finds something that brings back pleasant thoughts of another time and a very special person.

Some Things You Will Read About:

dune (dŭn)   a hill of loose sand piled up by the wind

reed (rēd)   tall grass with a long, hollow stem

sand (sand)   tiny bits of rock found on beaches and deserts

A Gift From the Sea

My nose told me it was almost supper time. I could smell something wonderful. Hamburgers over an open fire! It was getting late and many people had gone home. I climbed up a big rock to look out over the sea. Something out on the water caught my eye.

Reeds?

I looked some more. An old thought, clear and strong, came into my mind. I jumped down and ran toward the water.

"Hey, Reggie, what's up?" my friend Sparky called.

I walked out far enough to gather up the reeds. I pushed them closer to the beach. Some boys I knew, came over.

"Find what you're looking for, Reggie?" one of them joked.

I didn't answer.

"Let us know if you need any help," someone said, and they walked away.

I carried the reeds away from the water. Sparky grabbed an armful and followed me. Nearby, was a low sand dune. I placed the reeds near it. Then, I covered them with a lot of sand. Sparky did the same. I didn't say so, but I was glad for Sparky's help. It made me feel good.

My mind was full of thoughts and feelings I didn't know were there. Almost always, I did things by myself. I didn't like people around me all the time. But sometimes I needed someone to talk to—like now.

I sat down on the dune. Sparky sat down, too, and started to cover his legs with sand. "Sure wish I knew what this is all about," he said.

I laughed. "Seeing those reeds reminded me of my grandfather. I used to be afraid of the sea, so he took me for long, wonderful walks along the beach. We talked about things we saw. He said something good about everything — all sorts of stuff. One day, the whole beach was covered with broken 'sticks'. They were reeds. I asked him what they were."

"He told me, 'Every wave will carry this closer to the dune and push it under the sand.' Then he picked up one of the reeds and pulled it open. Inside were many little seeds.

"He said, 'The seeds will grow and next year we'll have good sea grass. We need that grass. The reeds will grow strong and they will hold the sand. And that helps the dune hold back the sea. But, the sea gives its gifts only once—be ready all the time.

"I didn't remember that, or him, until now."

"Think those seeds will take?" Sparky asked.

"I couldn't say. We'll have to come back next summer to see."

"Supper's ready!" someone called.

"Whoo-ee, let me at them." Sparky freed himself with one strong kick. I glanced at the spot where the reeds were.

"Hey, thanks for your help," I called. Then I followed the wonderful smell to supper.

A Gift From the Sea

COMPREHENSION CHECK

Preview Answer:
d.   Reggie and Sparky understand each other.

Choose the best answer.

1. Reggie and Sparky
    ____ a. pulled nets through the water.
    ____ b. planted reeds in the sand.
    ____ c. were fishing near the land.
    ____ d. put reeds into the water.

2. Reggie
    ____ a. always wanted people around him.
    ____ b. did not want Sparky's help.
    ____ c. wished that the other boys would join him.
    ____ d. was glad that Sparky helped him that day.

3. The reeds
    ____ a. grew in the woods.
    ____ b. had age rings.
    ____ c. were of little help to the dunes.
    ____ d. reminded Reggie of his grandfather.

4. To find out if the seeds would "take,"
    ____ a. the boys would have to come back in the fall.
    ____ b. the boys would have to come back next summer.
    ____ c. the boys would ask their teacher.
    ____ d. Reggie would ask his grandfather.

5. Inside the reeds there were
    ____ a. seeds.
    ____ b. age rings.
    ____ c. branches.
    ____ d. bugs.

6. Sea grass
    ____ a. grows on a farm.
    ____ b. helps hold the sand in its place.
    ____ c. does not come from reeds.
    ____ d. does not grow near the water.

7. The gifts of the sea were
    ____ a. just Reggie's dreams.
    ____ b. only fish and rocks.
    ____ c. very important to Reggie and his grandfather.
    ____ d. made and given by special people.

8. Reggie planted the reeds
    ____ a. to show Sparky what he knew.
    ____ b. just for something to do.
    ____ c. for a school class.
    ____ d. to remember his grandfather.

9. Another name for this story could be
    ____ a. "Learning About the Sea."
    ____ b. "A Grandfather's Gift."
    ____ c. "A Trip to the Beach."
    ____ d. "Making Friends at Sea."

10. This story is mainly about
    ____ a. planting reeds on the beach.
    ____ b. families enjoying their trip to the sea.
    ____ c. a special feeling and help from remembering.
    ____ d. boating and fishing in the summer.

Check your answers with the key on page 53.

Idea Starter: Can you think of any other gifts that nature "gives" us?

A Gift From the Sea

VOCABULARY CHECK

branch	need	smell	strong	supper	wonderful

I.   Fill in the blank in each sentence with the correct key word from the box above.

1.   The _____ of the cake floated through the house.

2.   We put our blanket down under the cover of a large _____ .

3.   The _____ man picked up the heavy chairs.

4.   I _____ new shoes for school.

5.   The birthday party was a _____ surprise.

6.   I set the table for _____ every night.

II.   Read each sentence. Check <u>Yes</u> if the sentence makes sense. Check <u>No</u> if the sentence does not make sense.

1.   A <u>branch</u> is a part of the body.   Yes _____   No _____

2.   <u>Supper</u> is a morning meal.   Yes _____   No _____

3.   People <u>need</u> food and water to live.   Yes _____   No _____

4.   We could <u>smell</u> the beautiful flowers
     in the garden.   Yes _____   No _____

5.   Someone is <u>strong</u> if they can lift
     heavy things.   Yes _____   No _____

6.   We had a <u>wonderful</u> time at the party.   Yes _____   No _____

Check your answers with the key on page 57.

This page may be reproduced for classroom use.

Being Brothers

Learn the Key Words

arm	(ärm)	the part of the body between your shoulder and hand *Gary broke his arm playing football.*
bad	(bad)	not good *The bad boy did not listen to his father.*
because	(bi kôz´)	to say why *He will win the prize because he is the best.*
early	(ėr´lē)	1. before time *Peggy is always early for school.* 2. the beginning part *Camp starts early this summer.*
food	(füd)	things to eat *The food for supper smelled good.*
shout	(shoůt)	to talk loud; to yell *Shout if someone is far away and can't hear you.*

Preview:

1. Read the title.
2. Look at the picture.
3. Read the first six paragraphs of the story.
4. Then answer the following question.

You learned from your preview that

_____ a. the boys were fighting when Mother called them.
_____ b. Billy fell down the stairs.
_____ c. Tommy never put his things away.
_____ d. Billy left his shoes on the step.

Turn to the Comprehension Check on page 34 for the right answer.

Now read the story.

Read to find out how two brothers get along.

Being Brothers

Having a brother is not always easy. When one brother is messy, things can sometimes get out of hand.

Something You Will Read About:

hamster (ham′stər)   a small animal with fur that likes to eat nuts and seeds

Being Brothers

Mother called Tommy and Billy for supper. The boys hurried down the stairs from their room.

"I will get there before you, Billy," said Tommy as he pushed his little brother out of the way.

"Oh, no you won't," said Billy.

They ran down the steps, but Tommy was faster than Billy. As he reached the last step, he saw Billy's shoes in the way. He could not stop and he fell over the shoes.

Tommy began to shout, "Why don't you put your shoes away? You never put any of your things away."

Billy shouted back to Tommy, "Why should I put them away when I am going to use them again?"

The food smelled good and Tommy was ready to eat. His father called to say he would be home late, so they were eating an early dinner.

"Mother, Billy is so bad about putting his things away—his paints and toys are all over."

"Well, after supper, you boys both go upstairs and clean up," their mother said.

"Why do I have to?" asked Tommy.

"Because Billy needs help this time. Next time, he will do it by himself."

After supper, Tommy put all of the toys away. Billy took his time putting away his clothes. That made Tommy angry. He told Billy they were going to have a long talk with their father, later.

Dad was not happy about Billy's messy ways. He told them he would talk to them in the morning. Then he helped the boys get ready for bed. Before Tommy went to bed, he always stopped to say "good night" to his hamster. Herbie, the hamster, stayed in a cage in their room. Tommy loved to play with Herbie. When it was time to give him food, Tommy would put a peanut in his pocket. Herbie would run up his arm and try to find the food.

Now, Tommy looked in the cage, but Herbie was not there.

"Did you see Herbie?" Tommy asked Billy.

"Yes," said Billy. "I was playing with him."

"Well, now you can help me find him!" shouted Tommy.

They looked all over the room, but no Herbie. Then, they heard a noise. It was coming from Billy's toy barn. Tommy put his arm in and Herbie crawled into his hand.

He said "good night" to his pet and put him in his cage.

"Now we can all go to sleep," said their mother.

Before their father put out the light, Billy asked, "Don't you think it was good that my barn wasn't put away? It helped us find Herbie."

"You were bad to let him out. But I guess, this time, I am glad that you did not put all your things away," said Tommy.

The next day, their father told them he had some good news. "In the early spring we will be moving to a big, new house. You will each have a room of your own."

Tommy was looking forward to having his own room.

Being Brothers

COMPREHENSION CHECK

Choose the best answer.

1. Tommy was angry at Billy because Billy
    _____ a. was not a friendly brother.
    _____ b. never put his things away.
    _____ c. was fresh to their mother.
    _____ d. thought Tommy was messy.

2. The boys and their mother were eating early, because
    _____ a. it was a Sunday afternoon.
    _____ b. their family had company.
    _____ c. their father was going to be home late.
    _____ d. they were going to clean up that night.

3. Billy
    _____ a. was always helpful around the house.
    _____ b. liked to help his brother.
    _____ c. listened to his mother.
    _____ d. did not do his part in cleaning up.

4. Herbie was
    _____ a. Tommy's hamster.
    _____ b. Billy's friend.
    _____ c. Tommy's brother.
    _____ d. Father's friend.

5. Herbie got lost
    _____ a. after Tommy fed him.
    _____ b. after Billy played with him.
    _____ c. before dinner.
    _____ d. after bedtime.

6. The boys
    _____ a. found Herbie in Billy's toy barn.
    _____ b. found Herbie the next day.
    _____ c. never found Herbie again.
    _____ d. got a new pet hamster.

7. Billy
    _____ a. said that he would never be mean again.
    _____ b. would not talk to Tommy after he was shouted at.
    _____ c. believed that leaving out his toy barn saved the day.
    _____ d. told his mother that Tommy had lost the hamster.

8. The good news that Dad told Tommy and Billy was that
    _____ a. they were going on a fun trip.
    _____ b. the boys would not have to clean up any more.
    _____ c. he bought them each a dog.
    _____ d. each boy would have a room of his own soon.

9. Another name for this story could be
    _____ a. "Finding a Hamster."
    _____ b. "Different Ways."
    _____ c. "Moving Away."
    _____ d. "An Early Dinner."

10. This story is mainly about
    _____ a. a lost hamster.
    _____ b. living together and sharing.
    _____ c. moving to a new house.
    _____ d. a kind father.

Check your answers with the key on page 53.

Idea Starter: Do you think it is better to have brothers or sisters or would you rather be an only child?

Being Brothers

VOCABULARY CHECK

arm	bad	because	early	food	shout

I.   Fill in the blank in each sentence with the correct key word from the box above.

1. My mother bought a lot of _____ at the store.

2. The _____ weather put an end to the game.

3. I had to _____ to my friend across the playground.

4. My _____ hurt after throwing the ball for a long time.

5. We always go out to play _____ on Saturday mornings.

6. I go to school _____ I like to read, write and play.

II.   Match the words with their meanings by writing the letter of the right meaning next to each word.

    _____ 1. bad   a. a part of your body

    _____ 2. shout   b. to say why

    _____ 3. arm   c. not good

    _____ 4. food   d. to yell

    _____ 5. because   e. before time

    _____ 6. early   f. things to eat

Check your answers with the key on page 58.

Summer With Rebecca

Learn the Key Words

finish	(fin′ ish)	to do something to the end *Can you finish your homework before bedtime?*
kitchen	(kich′ ə n)	a room where food is kept and meals are made *Grandma was in the kitchen making supper.*
later	(lāt′ ər)	after a while; not right now *Please come back to see me later.*

left	(left)	1. not taken
		   Jan's coat was left on the chair.
		2. past tense of leave
		   Carol left her house early.

poor	(pu̇r)	1. not having much money
		   The poor family lived in one room.
		2. unlucky
		   That poor man has broken a leg.

sign	(sīn)	1. something that tells us about a thing or person
		   Dark clouds are a sign of rain.
		2. a board with writing on it
		   The sign on the door said "Closed."

Preview:
1. Read the title.
2. Look at the picture.
3. Read the first six paragraphs of the story.
4. Then answer the following question.

You learned from your preview that
_____ a. Grandma was not a very good cook.
_____ b. Karen wanted to be somewhere else.
_____ c. Karen lived on a farm since she was very little.
_____ d. Karen's mother and father worked on a farm.
Turn to the Comprehension Check on page 39 for the right answer.

Now read the story.

Read to find out about Karen's new friend.

Summer With Rebecca

Karen is very sad on her grandparents' farm, until she meets Rebecca.

Something You Will Read About:

goat (gōt)   a small animal with horns, almost always found on farms

---

Summer With Rebecca

Grandmother's kitchen smelled wonderful. Karen watched Grandma bake a cake for supper. But, Karen felt sad. Her mother and father were far away in the city.

"Grandma," she said, "can I go home soon?"

Grandma turned around. Her face was kind.

"You asked Grandpa that last night, child. Is it so bad here on the farm?"

Karen liked the farm. "I like visiting you and Grandpa," she said. "But I miss Mom and Dad."

"Karen," said Grandma, "your mother and father work every day. They don't want you to be left alone. When school begins again in September, you will be back at home."

Karen stamped her foot. "Grandma! I'm eight years old. I'm not a baby!"

Just then, the kitchen door opened. In walked Grandpa.

"Do I hear my big, strong, city girl?" he said.

He sat down at the table beside Karen. "That's a sign that you will take good care of Rebecca," Grandpa said to Karen.

"Who is Rebecca?" asked Karen.

"Rebecca lives near us," said Grandpa. "Her mother is sick and Rebecca is still very little. Can you help take care of her?"

Karen seemed pleased with this new job and wanted to begin right away.

Grandma told her to wait. "When we finish supper, you can visit Rebecca."

Later, Grandpa and Karen went out. "Let's go to the barn," said Grandpa.

"But I want to visit Rebecca!" said Karen.

Grandpa smiled. In the barn, he pointed to a little white goat. "That's Rebecca. We feed her milk from a bottle because she is still a baby and her mother is very sick." He pointed to the bottle. "If she cries, it's a sign that she wants milk."

Karen petted Rebecca's soft, white back. "Or it's a sign that she misses her mother. Poor Rebecca."

Later that night, Karen heard Rebecca crying. She got out of bed and walked into the kitchen. It was very dark. Grandma and Grandpa were asleep now.

"Maaa!" The crying was very loud now.

Karen hurried out to the barn. The chickens were clucking, a cow was swinging its tail, and the old horse was stamping his foot. They did not like noises so late at night.

Karen filled the milk bottle. She put her arm around Rebecca's warm, white body and watched the little goat drink.

At last, the goat was finished.

"Good night, Rebecca," said Karen.

She patted the goat's head and went to the barn door. Rebecca walked behind her. She looked at Karen and her eyes begged, "Don't go."

"Poor thing," said Karen. "I'll be back later. I promise."

Karen left the barn, smiling. She did not think about going home anymore. Rebecca needed her.

Summer With Rebecca

COMPREHENSION CHECK

Choose the best answer.

1.   Karen
_____ a.   was spending the summer with her grandparents.
_____ b.   liked living in the country more than the city.
_____ c.   did not miss her parents.
_____ d.   felt very young.

2.   Karen's grandparents
_____ a.   lived in the city.
_____ b.   went to work every day.
_____ c.   lived on a farm.
_____ d.   did not like children.

3.   Rebecca needed care because
_____ a.   she had no mother.
_____ b.   her mother was sick.
_____ c.   she was always hungry.
_____ d.   she did not like the farm.

4.   Rebecca was
_____ a.   the little girl next door.
_____ b.   a big, fat cow.
_____ c.   Karen's sister.
_____ d.   a young, white goat.

5.   The goat
_____ a.   was fed milk from a baby bottle.
_____ b.   was not friendly to Rebecca.
_____ c.   was almost all grown up.
_____ d.   didn't mind being alone.

6.   When Karen heard Rebecca crying, she
_____ a.   called out to her grandparents.
_____ b.   cried, too.
_____ c.   went to the barn to feed her.
_____ d.   didn't help.

7.   Karen and Rebecca
_____ a.   both liked to drink milk.
_____ b.   felt the same way about their mothers.
_____ c.   did not like each other very much.
_____ d.   were not the same in any way.

8.   Karen wanted to stay on the farm because
_____ a.   she liked to plant corn.
_____ b.   it was fun to work the machines.
_____ c.   she believed that Rebecca needed her.
_____ d.   the horses needed riding.

9.   Another name for this story could be
_____ a.   "Life on the Farm."
_____ b.   "Back to the City."
_____ c.   "Rebecca's New Friend."
_____ d.   "Riding is Fun."

10.   This story is mainly about
_____ a.   life on the farm and all the work to be done.
_____ b.   a little girl finding out that animals can be lonely, too.
_____ c.   going to school in the big city.
_____ d.   a grandparent's visit to his granddaughter.

Check your answers with the key on page 53.

Idea Starter: What do you think would be better—living on a farm or in a big city?

Summer With Rebecca

VOCABULARY CHECK

finish	kitchen	later	left	poor	sign

I. Fill in the blank in each sentence with the correct key word from the box above.

1. Karen's smile was a _____ of her happiness.

2. The teacher asked us to _____ our work before lunchtime.

3. The _____ puppy missed its mother.

4. I went to the _____ to get a glass of milk.

5. Billy _____ his books at school and couldn't do his homework.

6. I will go to the playground _____ .

II. Use the words from the box above to fill in the puzzle.

Down
1. after a while
2. to do something to the end

Across
3. not taken
4. a room where meals are made
5. unlucky
6. something that tells about a thing or a person

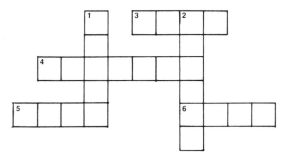

Check your answers with the key on page 58.

This page may be reproduced for classroom use.

BENJAMIN WEST

Learn the Key Words

dirty   (dėr′tē)   not clean
Alan was <u>dirty</u> from playing ball.

feather   (feŦH′ər)   part of the wing of a bird
The bird was all blue, but it had one white <u>feather</u>.

felt   (felt)   touched; to have had a feeling
Susan <u>felt</u> cold when she went out of her house.

great   (grāt)   very important; very good
The President of our country is a <u>great</u> man.

maybe   (mā′bē)   it may be
<u>Maybe</u> we can go to the park if it does not rain.

sheep   (shēp)   an animal raised for wool and food
The farmer had many <u>sheep</u>, cows, and horses.

Preview:

1. Read the title.
2. Look at the picture.
3. Read the first six paragraphs of the story.
4. Then answer the following question.

You learned from your preview that
_____ a. Benjamin learned how to make four colors.
_____ b. Great Bear showed Benjamin how to paint.
_____ c. Benjamin's first painting was of his cat.
_____ d. Benjamin showed Great Bear how to make a boat.
Turn to the Comprehension Check on page 44 for the right answer.

Now read the story.

Read to find out about the early years of a great American painter.

BENJAMIN WEST

As far back as he could think, Benjamin West had only one dream—to someday become a great painter.

Some People You Will Read About:
Indians (in′ dē ənz)   the first Americans

Some Places You Will Read About:
England (ing′ glənd)   a country in Europe
Philadelphia (fil ə del′ fē ə)   a city in Pennsylvania

BENJAMIN WEST

Benjamin West looked out the window of the farmhouse and said to his cat, "I wish we could go outside, but I must stay with little Sally."

He began to paint a picture of the sleeping baby. When his mother came home, she looked at the picture of her baby.

"This picture is very good, Benjamin," she said. "Now, you may go out and play. But don't get dirty."

Benjamin and his cat walked away from the farm. They found their Indian friend Great Bear. He was making a boat. Benjamin drew a picture of the Indian on the side of a tree. Great Bear looked at the picture and said, "You must have color."

He showed Benjamin how to make red and yellow colors from the earth.

That night, Benjamin showed his new colors to his mother. Then, she showed him how to make the color blue. Now he had three colors—red, blue, and yellow. The blue and yellow could make the color green, just like the spring grass.

Benjamin painted a picture of his father's sheep, with a feather. But the black paint would not stay on the feather. Then, he looked at the long tail of his cat. If he cut hair from the cat's tail, he could put it on the feather. His cat would not miss the hair.

With the cat's hair and his new paints, Benjamin could paint the sheep, cows, horses and many other things around the farm.

One day, his Uncle John from Philadelphia came to visit. He liked Benjamin's paintings very much.

"These paintings are very good, Benjamin," he said. "I would like this painting of the flowers for my home."

Benjamin was happy to give the picture to Uncle John.

Benjamin worked on the farm all day and painted pictures at night. One night, his father came in just as he was cutting hair from the cat's tail.

"You must not cut the cat's hair for your feathers," he said.

Benjamin felt sad. He could not paint without the cat's hair. When he saw the new spring flowers, he wanted to paint again. As he worked on the farm each day, he saw things he wanted to paint.

Benjamin was playing with the sheep one morning when a wagon pulled up.

"I have a box from Philadelphia for Benjamin West," the man said.

Benjamin ran to open the box. It was very dirty on the outside.

"It's a paint box from Uncle John, with paints and pictures in it!" he shouted.

He looked at the pictures in the box and said, "Maybe I could paint like this, someday."

That night, Benjamin went to bed with his cat and his new paint box. He could not sleep because he felt so happy. Maybe he would be a great painter someday.

His wish came true and when Benjamin West grew older, he did become a great painter. He went to England where he became a painter for the King.

BENJAMIN WEST

COMPREHENSION CHECK

Choose the best answer.

1. Benjamin liked to
   ____ a. work on the farm.
   ____ b. paint pictures.
   ____ c. care for babies.
   ____ d. help his mother.

2. This story takes place
   ____ a. in the city.
   ____ b. on the sea.
   ____ c. on a farm.
   ____ d. in a zoo.

3. Great Bear
   ____ a. did not like Benjamin's paintings.
   ____ b. thought it was silly to paint on a tree.
   ____ c. was too busy with his boat to help Benjamin.
   ____ d. helped Benjamin learn to mix colors.

4. In order to get the paint to stick to the feather, Benjamin
   ____ a. used some hair from his cat's tail.
   ____ b. used some glue.
   ____ c. put a lot of paint on the brush.
   ____ d. used some grass.

5. Benjamin's father
   ____ a. bought him a painting set.
   ____ b. would not let him use the cat's hair.
   ____ c. did not like him to paint.
   ____ d. liked Benjamin's pictures.

6. Benjamin's Uncle John.
   ____ a. did not think that Benjamin's paintings were good.
   ____ b. wanted Benjamin to go to Philadelphia.
   ____ c. sent Benjamin a paint set and pictures.
   ____ d. thought that painting was a silly thing.

7. As a child, Benjamin West
   ____ a. was a good painter.
   ____ b. did not listen to his father.
   ____ c. was a terrible painter.
   ____ d. never wanted to be great.

8. When Benjamin grew older, he
   ____ a. bought a farm and planted lots of corn.
   ____ b. went to the city to study.
   ____ c. gave away his old cat.
   ____ d. went to England and painted for the King.

9. Another name for this story could be
   ____ a. "Indian Ways."
   ____ b. "Making Boats."
   ____ c. "The Will to Paint."
   ____ d. "Learning to Farm."

10. This story is mainly about
    ____ a. a kind and friendly uncle.
    ____ b. a young boy's strong longing to paint.
    ____ c. how Indians helped the white man.
    ____ d. working on a farm.

Check your answers with the key on page 53.

Idea Starter: How many other famous men or women can you think of?

This page may be reproduced for classroom use.

BENJAMIN WEST

VOCABULARY CHECK

dirty	feather	felt	great	maybe	sheep

I.   Fill in the blank in each sentence with the correct key word from the box above.

1. I _____ warm sitting by the fire.

2. We put the _____ clothes in the wash.

3. The _____ were eating grass in the fields.

4. My shirt was as white as a duck's _____ .

5. Our school has a _____ band.

6. _____ we can play outside after lunch.

II.   Match the words with the right meanings by writing the letter of the meaning on the line next to the key word.

Column A	Column B
____ 1. maybe	a. not clean
____ 2. feather	b. very important
____ 3. dirty	c. it may be
____ 4. great	d. to have had a feeling
____ 5. sheep	e. something found on birds
____ 6. felt	f. an animal raised for wool

Check your answers with the key on page 59.

BOBBY'S WISH

Learn the Key Words

hope	(hōp)	a strong wish for something *I hope to win the foot race on Saturday.*
jolly	(jol´ē)	full of fun; happy *There were many jolly people at the circus.*
lion	(lī´ən)	a big wild animal belonging to the cat family *We saw a lion and his family at the zoo.*
sky	(skī)	the air above the earth *The sky was blue and the birds sang in the trees.*
song	(sông)	words and music together *We sang a song about going on a picnic.*
stairs	(sterz)	a set of steps going from one floor to another *There are no stairs in our house.*

Preview:

1. Read the title.
2. Look at the picture.
3. Read the first four paragraphs of the story.
4. Then answer the following question.

You learned from your preview that
_____ a. Bobby got two gifts from his parents.
_____ b. Bobby's parents were going to buy circus candy for him.
_____ c. Bobby did not really care about going to the circus.
_____ d. Bobby's parents were taking him to the circus for his birthday.

Turn to the Comprehension Check on page 49 for the right answer.

Now read the story.

Read to find out about a special birthday surprise.

BOBBY'S WISH

When his birthday finally comes, Bobby gets a very pleasant surprise.

Something You Will Read About:

elephant (el′ ə fənt) a large, wild animal with a long nose called a trunk. Elephants are seen at zoos and circuses.

BOBBY'S WISH

Bobby looked up from his book. It was all about the circus. More than anything else, he wished that he could go to the circus. But his mother and father did not have the money to buy tickets. They lived on a farm and worked very hard to make a living.

One day as Bobby was walking home from school, he saw a big sign. It said that the circus was coming to town—the same day as his birthday.

Soon the big day came. Bobby still did not have a ticket to get into the circus. When he woke up that morning, he got dressed and ran down the stairs. His parents gave him a racing car set and a model airplane. But Bobby could only think about the circus. He ran up the stairs to put away his new things. Then, he walked to where the circus tents were being put up.

The sky was as blue as a bluebird, and the birds were all singing a happy song.

Bobby saw some men putting up tents. When he asked if he could help, the men let him pull the ropes with them. They all thanked him for his help.

Then, Bobby saw some men getting their wagons ready. Some had balloons, one had peanuts and another had ice cream. One jolly man gave Bobby a candy apple.

Soon, it was time for the animals to have their lunch. When Bobby came to the elephants' cage, the man asked him if he would like to help feed them. This was more than Bobby could hope for. He gave them some straw and peanuts. Bobby and the man laughed as one elephant made a funny noise.

Then, Bobby came to the lions' cage. It was the first time Bobby had seen such animals. He was only used to seeing farm animals like cows and horses and ducks. Bobby stepped back as the lion let out a loud roar. Bobby talked to the lion trainer for a long time. Then he thanked him for his time and walked over to the clowns' tent.

Bobby watched the clowns carefully. They were such a jolly group of men. They made each other laugh as they did their work. One of the clowns put some make-up on Bobby. Another dressed him in a funny hat and baggy pants.

Soon, it was time for Bobby to go home and eat his dinner. One of the clowns said that he had a surprise for Bobby. He gave him three tickets for the circus that night! It was the clowns' way of thanking Bobby for all his help that day. Again, this was more than Bobby could have hoped for. It was the best thing that anyone could have given him for his birthday. Bobby was so happy, he could have jumped as high as the sky.

Bobby ran home to tell his mother and father. All the way home, Bobby sang a song. "Happy birthday to me, happy birthday to me . . ."

BOBBY'S WISH

COMPREHENSION CHECK

Preview Answer:
a.   Bobby got two gifts from his parents.

Choose the best answer.

1. Bobby's parents gave him
   _____ a.   a model car and tickets to the circus.
   _____ b.   money to buy circus tickets.
   _____ c.   a racing car set and model airplane.
   _____ d.   a blue bird.

2. Bobby's parents
   _____ a.   did not have the money to take him to the circus.
   _____ b.   did not want to go to the circus.
   _____ c.   thought that the circus was a waste of money.
   _____ d.   did not really care about Bobby's birthday.

3. Bobby got the tickets from
   _____ a.   a clown.
   _____ b.   the circus owner.
   _____ c.   the lion tamer.
   _____ d.   the men putting up the tents.

4. Before he got the tickets, Bobby was
   _____ a.   happy, but disappointed.
   _____ b.   sad and angry.
   _____ c.   mad at his parents.
   _____ d.   crying.

5. Bobby
   _____ a.   did not like to help people.
   _____ b.   was a selfish little boy.
   _____ c.   wanted to leave home and join the circus.
   _____ d.   wanted to go to the circus for his birthday.

6. Bobby fed the elephants
   _____ a.   ice cream.
   _____ b.   straw and peanuts.
   _____ c.   candy apples and bananas.
   _____ d.   some of his birthday cake.

7. When Bobby heard the lion roar, he
   _____ a.   stepped toward the cage.
   _____ b.   laughed with the lion trainer.
   _____ c.   moved back in fear.
   _____ d.   roared back.

8. The clowns were
   _____ a.   funny and friendly.
   _____ b.   sad and mean.
   _____ c.   making fun of Bobby.
   _____ d.   all dressed the same.

9. Another name for this story could be
   _____ a.   "Bobby Becomes a Circus Star."
   _____ b.   "Clowning Around."
   _____ c.   "What the Circus is Really Like."
   _____ d.   "A Very Happy Birthday."

10. This story is mainly about
    _____ a.   how wishes come true.
    _____ b.   a little boy who gets his birthday wish.
    _____ c.   a selfish little boy.
    _____ d.   what circus people are really like.

Check your answers with the key on page 53.

Idea Starter: What special wishes do you have?

VOCABULARY CHECK

| hope | jolly | lion | sky | song | stairs |

I. **Fill in the blank in each sentence with the correct key word from the box above.**

1. There was not a cloud in the _____ .
2. The _____ old man always bought us ice cream.
3. My mother sings a special _____ when she works in the garden.
4. I _____ that I get a red bicycle for my birthday.
5. The _____ roared and scared the children.
6. Jackie fell down the _____ in her house.

II. **Find the hidden words in the letters below. They may be written from left to right or up and down. One word, that is not a key word, has been done for you.**

L	O	S	T	K	I	T	E	N	A
I	N	S	T	A	I	R	S	U	P
O	P	E	N	T	A	N	D	R	F
N	E	F	T	J	O	L	L	Y	L
S	D	A	Y	S	H	P	T	S	C
O	A	D	R	G	O	T	P	K	N
N	J	C	H	I	P	D	G	Y	U
G	M	O	U	T	E	B	R	A	R
S	U	P	L	A	A	I	O	N	E
T	Y	G	R	A	E	D	O	P	L

Check your answers with the key on page 59.

This page may be reproduced for classroom use.

KEY WORDS
Lessons B-1 - B-10

B-1

brother
carry
drop
land
sent
wear

B-2

cage
done
drive
follow
fox
knock

B-3

family
reach
stand
threw
wait
write

B-4

drink
face
foot
kind
king
love

B-5

band
crawl
listen
visit
whale
world

B-6

branch
need
smell
strong
supper
wonderful

KEY WORDS
Lessons B-1 - B-10

B-7

arm
bad
because
early
food
shout

B-8

finish
kitchen
later
left
poor
sign

B-9

dirty
feather
felt
great
maybe
sheep

B-10

hope
jolly
lion
sky
song
stairs

COMPREHENSION CHECK ANSWER KEY
Lessons B-1 - B-10

LESSON NUMBER	QUESTION NUMBER										PAGE NUMBER
	1	2	3	4	5	6	7	8	9	10	
B-1	a	ⓒ	b	d	b	a	b	ⓑ	△c	[a]	4
B-2	a	b	c	a	d	ⓑ	ⓓ	b	△a	[c]	9
B-3	ⓓ	a	c	a	ⓑ	c	a	a	△a	[d]	14
B-4	a	b	d	ⓒ	c	d	b	a	△a	[b]	19
B-5	b	c	d	b	a	ⓐ	b	ⓓ	△c	[b]	24
B-6	b	d	d	b	a	b	c	ⓓ	△b	[c]	29
B-7	b	c	d	a	b	a	ⓒ	d	△b	[b]	34
B-8	a	c	b	d	a	c	ⓑ	c	△c	[b]	39
B-9	b	c	d	a	b	c	ⓐ	d	△c	[b]	44
B-10	c	a	a	ⓐ	d	b	c	a	△d	[b]	49

Code: ◯ = Inference

△ = Another Name for the Story

▢ = Main Idea

NOTES

VOCABULARY CHECK ANSWER KEY
Lessons B-1 - B-10

B-1   THREE JOBS FOR THREE BROTHERS   5

I.
1. drop
2. sent
3. carry
4. wear
5. brother
6. land

II.

B-2   THE FOX SHOW   10

I.
1. cage
2. follow
3. drive
4. fox
5. done
6. knock

II.

C	A	G	E	M	O	P	S
Z	E	B	R	A	T	O	O
D	S	F	O	X	A	B	C
R	T	O	U	N	D	E	R
I	B	L	M	S	E	N	K
V	I	L	K	A	A	U	N
E	A	O	P	L	U	N	O
B	P	W	D	O	N	E	C
A	C	E	R	T	L	A	K

VOCABULARY CHECK ANSWER KEY
Lessons B-1 - B-10

B-3   **GETTING TO KNOW EACH OTHER**

I.
1. family
2. write
3. reach
4. stand
5. threw
6. wait

II.
1. wait
2. write
3. stand
4. reach
5. threw
6. family

B-4   **THE UNICORN**

I.
1. face
2. kind
3. drink
4. king
5. foot
6. love

II.
1. yes
2. no
3. no
4. yes
5. yes
6. yes

VOCABULARY CHECK ANSWER KEY
Lessons B-1 - B-10

LESSON NUMBER		PAGE NUMBER

B-5   **A WHALE OF A TALE**   25

I. 1. whale   *II.* 1. c
2. listen   2. a
3. crawl   3. e
4. band   4. d
5. visit   5. f
6. world   6. b

B-6   **A GIFT FROM THE SEA**   30

I. 1. smell   *II.* 1. no
2. branch   2. no
3. strong   3. yes
4. need   4. yes
5. wonderful   5. yes
6. supper   6. yes

VOCABULARY CHECK ANSWER KEY
Lessons B-1 - B-10

B-7   **BEING BROTHERS**   35

I.
1. food
2. bad
3. shout
4. arm
5. early
6. because

II.
1. c
2. d
3. a
4. f
5. b
6. e

B-8   **SUMMER WITH REBECCA**   40

I.
1. sign
2. finish
3. poor
4. kitchen
5. left
6. later

II.

VOCABULARY CHECK ANSWER KEY
Lessons B-1 - B-10

B-9   **BENJAMIN WEST**   45

I. 1. felt   *II.* 1. c
2. dirty   2. e
3. sheep   3. a
4. feather   4. b
5. great   5. f
6. maybe   6. d

B-10   **BOBBY'S WISH**   50

I. 1. sky
2. jolly
3. song
4. hope
5. lion
6. stairs

II.

L	O	S	T	K	I	T	E	N	A
I	N	S	T	A	I	R	S	U	P
O	P	E	N	T	A	N	D	R	F
N	E	F	T	J	O	L	L	Y	L
S	D	A	Y	S	H	P	T	S	C
O	A	D	R	G	O	T	P	K	N
N	J	C	H	I	P	D	G	Y	U
G	M	O	U	T	E	B	R	A	R
S	U	P	L	A	A	I	O	N	E
T	Y	G	R	A	E	D	O	P	L

NOTES